D0535685

iMath
Readers

A Toy Store Summer:
Finding Area

by John Perritano

ecialist

PRESS

Norwood House Press
PO Box 316598
Chicago, IL 60631

For information regarding Norwood House Press, please visit our website at
www.norwoodhousepress.com or call 866-565-2900.

Special thanks to: Heidi Doyle
Production Management: Six Red Marbles
Editors: Linda Bullock and Kendra Muntz
Printed in Heshan City, Guangdong, China. 208N—012013

Library of Congress Cataloging-in-Publication Data

Perritano, John.

  A toy store summer : finding area/by John Perritano; content consultant David
  Hughes, mathematics curriculum specialist.
  p. cm.—(iMath)

  Audience: 8–10.
  Audience: Grade 4 to 6.

  Summary: "The mathematical concept of area is introduced as a girl works
  at her first job collecting toys from a toy store warehouse. Readers learn two
  methods to find area: using an array to count square units, and using a formula
  for length times width. This book also includes a discover activity, connection
  to history, and mathematical vocabulary introduction"– Provided by publisher.

Includes bibliographical references and index.

ISBN 978-1-59953-565-4 (library edition: alk. paper)
ISBN 978-1-60357-534-8 (ebook)

1. Area measurement—Juvenile literature. 2. Toy stores—Juvenile literature. I. Title.

QA465.P47 2013
516'.154—dc23
2012034236

CONTENTS

Note to Caregivers:

Throughout this book, many questions are posed to the reader. Some are open-ended and ask what the reader thinks. Discuss these questions with your child and guide him or her in thinking through the possible answers and outcomes. There are also questions posed which have a specific answer. Encourage your child to read through the text to determine the correct answer. Most importantly, encourage answers grounded in reality while also allowing imaginations to soar. Information to help support you as you share the book with your child is provided in the back in the **Additional Notes** section.

Bold words are defined in the glossary in the back of the book.

Totally Toys

Tara had just finished her first day of work. She was excited to be earning money. She could go to the movies with her friends this weekend. She could save money for a new pair of blue jeans, too.

Tara wasn't the only person who was happy about her job. So were Monica, her little sister, and their cousin, Josh. Monica and Josh hoped Tara would take them to work with her so they could see the different kinds of toys! Tara's summer job was at Totally Toys, a huge new toy store. The store sold all kinds of games and toys. Board games. Pedal cars. Bicycles. Video games. Stuffed animals. The store was crammed to the ceiling with toys.

Covering Area

Totally Toys has a warehouse. That's where Tara works. She collects the toys that customers order online. Tara uses a map of the warehouse to find where each toy is located.

Monica asked her sister, "What's it like to work for a toy store, Tara?"

"It's harder than I thought it would be," Tara said. "We ship a lot of toys all over the world."

"Like where?" Josh asked.

"Well, today I collected 150 game sets to send to a school in Kenya, Africa."

"I took the game sets off a shelf. Then, I put them on trays. Next, I carried the trays to a **conveyor belt**. The belt carried the trays to the shipping department. That's where workers box and ship the orders," Tara explained.

"I wasn't sure how many game sets to put on each tray. So, Ms. Webster, my boss, showed me. You can think of each tray as a **plane figure**. It is a surface with length and width. The number of **square units** it takes to cover the surface is a tray's **area**. But none of the units can overlap."

"Ms. Webster showed me two different ways to find area," Tara said.

Idea 1: Count Square Units. "First, she showed me how to count square units to find area. She gave me some tiles. They were all the same size. Each tile, Ms. Webster said, represented a square unit."

"I used the square units to make an **array**. I made three rows of units, with the same number of units in each row. I counted the units. The tray had an area of 15 square units."

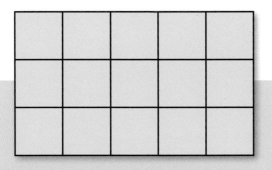

Is making an array a good way to find the area of a surface? Why or why not?

"I learned another way to find area, too."

Idea 2: Use a Formula. "I can use the **formula** $\ell \times w$ to find area. The ℓ stands for length. The w stands for width."

"What units do you use to measure?" asked Josh.

"I can use **metric units of length**. They include centimeters and decimeters. But everything we sell is measured in **customary units of length**. Those include inches and feet."

"For example, one of the trays I used measured 12 inches wide and 10 inches long. Its area was 120 square inches."

$$\begin{array}{r} 12 \text{ inches} \\ \times\ 10 \text{ inches} \\ \hline 120 \text{ square inches} \end{array}$$

Is using a formula a good way to find area? Why or why not?

8

Idea 3: Add areas. "I learned something else about using a formula to find area," Tara said. "Let's say that I have two or more trays. I can find the area of the surface of each tray. Then, I can add the areas together. That tells me how much area the trays have in all."

"That's cool," said Monica. "So, it doesn't matter how many trays you have. You can find a total area for all of them."

"That's right," said Tara. "So, let's say one tray measures 3 feet by 2 feet. Another tray measures 4 feet by 1 foot."

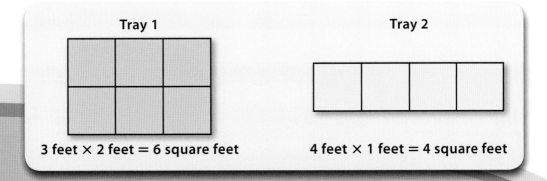

Tray 1   Tray 2

3 feet × 2 feet = 6 square feet   4 feet × 1 feet = 4 square feet

"I can add the areas together to find the total area of both trays."

$$\begin{array}{r} 6 \text{ square feet} \\ + 4 \text{ square feet} \\ \hline 10 \text{ square feet} \end{array}$$

Is adding areas a good way to find total area? Why or why not?

DISCOVER ACTIVITY

Materials

- a square pad of sticky notes
- a ruler or yardstick
- paper
- pen or pencil

Tile It

Plane figures are all around you. They are in your classroom and in your home. They are outside on the playground and in your neighborhood. You can find the area of any plane figure you see.

Make a chart like the one below. Find objects in your classroom or home that have square or rectangular surfaces. List the objects in the chart.

Object	Number of Unit Tiles	Area (in square units)

Then, use sticky notes as unit tiles. Use the tiles to cover the surface of each object in your list. Count the total number of square units. Write the area of each surface in square units.

Now, make a new chart and go outside. Look for square or rectangular objects or spaces. List what you find in your chart.

Next, use a ruler or yardstick to measure the length and width of each surface. Write your measurements in the chart. Then, use the formula $\ell \times w$ to find the area of the surface.

Object or Space	Length (in inches or feet)	Width (in inches or feet)	Area (in square inches or feet)

The Second Day at Work

On her next day of work, Tara had lots of toys to collect and lots of trays to fill. She read the list Ms. Webster had printed for her. The list included a map of the shelves, so Tara would know where to find the toys she needed. Tara pushed a cart to the shelves and began collecting toys. The first four orders on her list were toy rockets, model cars, puppets, and something strange called chattering teeth.

All of the toys Tara collected came in individual boxes. Tara decided to use each box as a unit. She arranged the boxes in arrays.

She started with one toy. She made a row of toy boxes. She wanted to put the greatest number of boxes possible on a single tray. That would save time and make it easier for the people in the shipping department.

Tara arranged the boxes holding toy rockets first. She made an array of three rows, with three rockets in each row. The boxes fit perfectly. Tara carried the tray to the conveyor belt and sent it on its way to shipping.

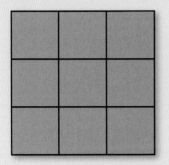

What is the area of the tray?

 **Did You Know?**

Did you know that some toys are called retro toys? These retro toys are brand new, but look like they were made many years ago.

Model Cars

The next array Tara made was with toy cars. Tara removed the boxes holding individual toy cars from her cart. She examined one box closely. Then, she chose a tray that she thought might work well. Her first choice was close. But her second choice was much better.

The array Tara built held ten rows with 20 boxes in each row.

What is the area of the tray that Tara filled?

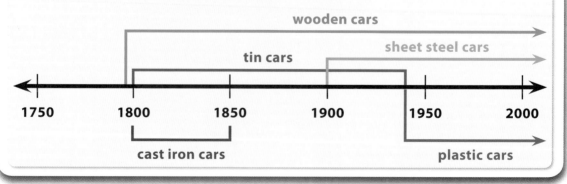

? Did You Know?

In the 1950s, a toymaker made a tiny metal car for his daughter. The car fit inside a matchbox. It gave the toymaker an idea. He and a friend began to make and sell toy cars small enough to fit inside a matchbox. The company has sold billions of these small cars.

History of Popular Toy Cars

wooden cars

sheet steel cars

tin cars

| 1750 | 1800 | 1850 | 1900 | 1950 | 2000 |

cast iron cars

plastic cars

Puppets, Puppets, Puppets

Next, Tara had to send hand puppets to shipping. She peeked inside each box, laughing at the soft toys she saw.

Tara paused and looked around. Everyone was working so quickly to fill toy orders. Tara thought she should work faster. She grabbed the first empty tray she found. The tray was three feet long and had an area of six square feet. What was the tray's perimeter? **Perimeter** is the distance all the way around an object.

Tara filled the tray but had puppet boxes left over. So, she took a second tray that was two feet wide and had an area of four square feet. What was the perimeter of the second tray? How much area did both trays have together?

Novelty Toys

Tara read an order for 120 chattering teeth. She had no idea what they were. But she knew from the map where she could find them.

One shelf held 15 boxes marked **"novelty toys."** Tara read the labels more closely. She found that each box held 120 toys. One box held jumping sports balls. Another held monkeys that flipped. A third box held begging dogs.

The fourth box was marked "walking brains." Tara couldn't imagine enjoying a toy like that. She was glad she wasn't filling an order for those.

The next box was the box she needed. She wondered if she could put this box directly on the conveyor belt. An open window separated the warehouse from the shipping department. Would the box fit through the window?

Tara measured the window. It measured 4 feet by 3 feet. She used the formula $\ell \times w$ to find the area.

What is the area of the opening?

Next, Tara looked at the box filled with chattering teeth. She determined which surface was the largest. Then, she measured it. The sides of the box were larger than the top and bottom. So, Tara measured one side. It measured 24 inches wide and 36 inches long. She used a formula to find the area of the surface.

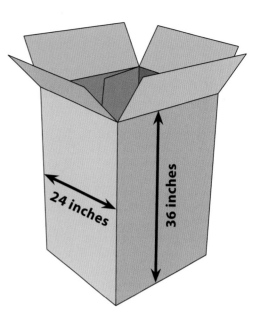

24 inches

36 inches

What is the area of the box's largest surface? Hint: Change inches to feet before you multiply. That will make it easier to compare areas.

Will the box of chattering teeth fit through the window?

Teddy Bears to Go

Tara really liked her next order. A children's hospital had ordered 128 teddy bears for their young patients. She thought it might take a while to collect 128 bears. Tara found the boxes and read one of the labels. Each box held 16 teddy bears, each in its own gift box.

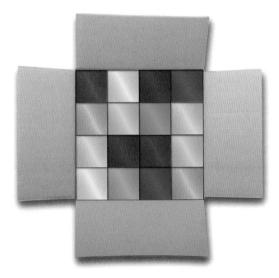

Tara measured the area of the top of the box. It measured 4 feet long and 4 feet wide.

What was the area of the surface of the box?

Next, Tara opened the box to see the array of gift boxes inside. There were four rows of four boxes.

What was the area of the top of one gift box? Hint: Use the area of the larger box to help you determine the area of each gift box in the array.

As Tara shipped the order, she remembered the story of how teddy bears were invented.

This statue of President Theodore Roosevelt stands in Washington, D.C.

Connecting to History

Theodore, or "Teddy," Roosevelt was the 26th president of the United States. He was also a hunter.

Some people on a bear hunt with the president found an elderly and sick bear. They invited the president to shoot it. But Roosevelt said there was no sport in killing a bear that was ill.

An artist named Clifford Berryman heard the story. He drew a cartoon of the event for the newspapers. He drew the bear many times, as he followed the president's career. He made the bear smaller and younger. This cartoon led to today's teddy bear.

Two important events happened that led to the toys we call teddy bears. One happened in the United States. The other happened in Germany.

In the United States, Morris Michtom saw Mr. Berryman's cartoons. Michtom owned a shop. He put two stuffed bears his wife had made in his shop window. Then, he wrote to President Roosevelt. He wanted permission to call the stuffed bears "Teddy's bears." The president agreed.

Meanwhile, in Germany, Margarete Steiff also made toys. Her nephew Richard joined her company. He bought special soft fabric to make a bear. He showed the bear at a toy fair in 1903. An American businessman ordered 3,000 of them!

Today, lots of people make and sell teddy bears. There are even teddy bear fairs. People come to buy bears and learn how to make them.

A Game of Checkers

Monica and Josh were playing a board game when Tara came home from her second day at work. Tara stopped before going upstairs to change out of her work clothes. "I collected lots of board games today," she said. "I'll tell you about it in a minute. Let me change first."

When Tara came back downstairs, Josh had a question for her. "The kids at school are talking about a new game," he told her. "I think it's called 'Zombies Take Revenge.' Did you collect any of those?" he asked.

Tara laughed. "No," she said. "I don't know that game. Today, I collected 200 checker sets."

"Wow!" exclaimed Monica. "Who wants 200 checker sets?"

"They're going to a group of neighborhood community centers, I think," Tara answered. "Each game comes with a rule book. The book begins with a history of checkers. I read it during my lunch break. Did you know that checkers is one of the oldest games ever played?" Tara asked.

The map pin points to Iraq.

"Are you sure?" asked Josh. "I thought chess was the oldest game."

"Well, chess is old, too. But it's not as old as checkers. This book talked about how **archaeologists** look for clues about how people lived in the past. Sometimes, those clues are buried beneath our feet! So, archaeologists dig up sites and study what they find. They found a 5,000-year-old checkerboard and game pieces! The board and pieces were buried in southern Iraq," Tara said.

"I'll be right back," Monica called, as she ran from the room.

Monica returned with a box in her hands. She took out a checkerboard. Checkers tumbled out and onto the table.

"The checker sets I collected today aren't as fancy as ours. But ours is a good model. I can use it to share with you what I learned. Look closely at the board. It has eight rows, and there are eight square units in each row. The pattern is an array. You can count the square units to find the board's area, or you can use a formula."

What is the area of the entire checkered space in square units?

"Now," Tara continued. "The squares on our checkerboard each measure two inches by two inches."

What is the area of one square?

What is the area of the entire checkered space in square inches?

Box It Up

At work the next day, Tara had a long list of toys to collect. The first item on her list was a single toy. It was for a pedal car.

Tara used her map to find the toy. When she found it, the box wasn't quite as large as she had expected. She read the label closely. It had a diagram of the box, with its measurements of length in inches.

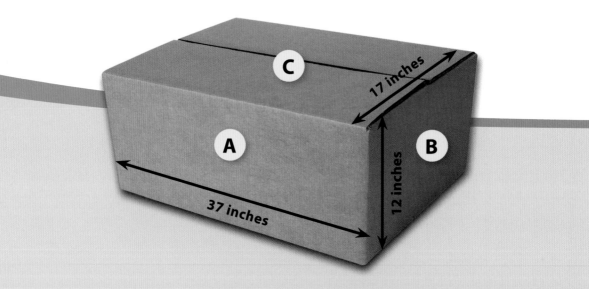

What is the area of the side of the box marked A?
What is the area of the side of the box marked B?
What is the area of the side of the box marked C?
What is the total surface area of the box?

Math at Work

A warehouse is often one huge room filled with shelves. The shelves can go from the ground to the ceiling. Some warehouse managers wrap groups of boxes in plastic. This helps to prevent them from slipping. Other managers buy warehouse nets. They wrap the nets around shelves to keep boxes from falling.

Workers measure the length of each shelf to know how many yards of net to buy. The company that makes the nets cuts and ships exact lengths.

The nets are flexible. They can bend and roll. Some companies make nets with grids. The area of each grid may be 1.5 square inches. The small area helps keep products where they belong.

This worker is driving a forklift. He uses prongs on the front of the machine to lift and lower boxes.

By the end of her third day of work, Tara had collected hundreds and hundreds of toys. They included board games, dolls, sets of building blocks, car models, remote-control airplanes, and even the parts of a playhouse. But her favorite toy of all was a stuffed giraffe.

An animal park ordered 10 giant stuffed giraffes for their gift shop. Each giraffe came in an enormous box.

Even the largest cart in the warehouse was not big enough to hold all ten boxes at once. Tara made more than one trip.

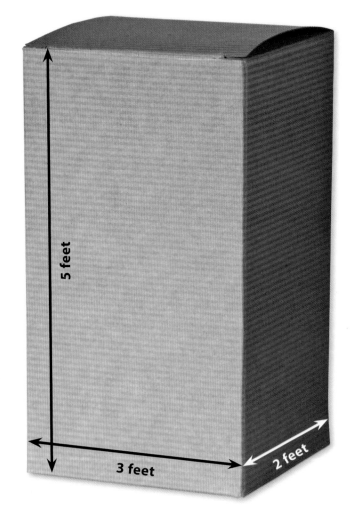

On her first trip, Tara loaded four boxes on a flat cart. The boxes were too tall to stand upright. She couldn't see over them. So, she put them on their sides. Two boxes fit on the bottom. Two more fit on top. Look at the diagram below. It shows what Tara saw when she stood at one end of the cart.

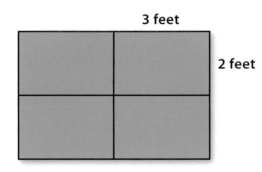

3 feet

2 feet

What is the surface area of the end of one box? What is the total surface area of the ends of all four boxes? How can Tara find out?

Idea 1: Count Square Units.
Tara could use an **array** to find area. She could cover each box end with square tiles. Then, she could count all of the tiles to find the total surface area. But Tara doesn't have enough tiles to find the area this way, and it would take a long time, even if she did.

27

Idea 2: Use a Formula. Tara could use the **formula** $\ell \times w$ to find the area of each end of each box. But, this will solve only part of the problem.

Idea 3: Add Areas. Tara could use the formula $\ell \times w$ to find the area of each end of each box. Then, she could **add the areas** to find the total surface area. This will solve both parts of the problem.

What is the total surface area of the ends of all four boxes?

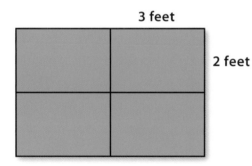

3 feet

2 feet

Tara solved the problem and smiled. She had learned a lot in only three days. She looked forward to a long summer filled with toys.

WHAT COMES NEXT?

Some people collect **vintage toys**. Vintage toys are old toys, sometimes found in antique shops and online.

Visit a library or go online with an adult. Look for examples of the kinds of vintage toys people enjoy collecting. You may find action figures, space toys, cars and trucks, robots, tiny animals, and teddy bears. Which toys interest you most?

Use a ruler to design a display box for your favorite toys. The box should have one section for each toy. Think of creative ways to arrange the toys. Share your design with a friend. Together, design another display box to hold some vintage toys you would both like to own.

GLOSSARY

archaeologist: a scientist who studies where and how people lived long ago.

area: the total number of square units that cover a surface.

array: a pattern of rows with an equal number of units in each row.

conveyor belt: a belt, chain, or set of rollers that carry objects from one part of a building to another.

customary units of length: a system of measures used in the United States. Customary units of length include inches, feet, yards, and miles.

formula: a mathematical rule, usually expressed in symbols.

metric units of length: a system of measures that is based on tens. Metric units of length include millimeters, centimeters, decimeters, meters, and kilometers.

novelty toys: toys that are small and inexpensive.

perimeter: the distance around an object.

plane figure: a two-dimensional figure, meaning it has length and width.

square units: units, such as inches and feet, used to measure area.

vintage toys: old toys from the past.

FURTHER READING

NONFICTION

Pack It Up: Surface Area and Volume, by Chloe Lane, Teacher Created Materials, 2012

Theodore Roosevelt for Kids, by Kerrie Logan Hollihan, Chicago Review Press, 2010

FICTION

Mr. Magorium's Wonder Emporium, by N.E. Bode, Scholastic, 2007

Winnie-the-Pooh, by A.A. Milne, Puffin Books, 2005

ADDITIONAL NOTES

The page references below provide answers to questions asked throughout the book. Questions whose answers will vary are not addressed.

Page 13: The area of the tray equals 9 rocket boxes.

Page 14: The area of the tray equals 200 toy car boxes.

Page 15: The perimeter of the first tray is 10 feet. The perimeter of the second tray is 8 feet. The combined area is 10 square feet (ft^2).

Page 16: 4 feet × 3 feet = 12 square feet

Page 17: 6 square feet. Yes, the box will fit through the window.

Page 18: 4 feet × 4 feet = 16 square feet; 16 square feet ÷ 16 boxes = 1 square foot per box

Page 23: 8 units × 8 units = 64 square units; 2 inches × 2 inches = 4 square inches; 16 inches × 16 inches = 256 square inches

Page 24: Area of A = 37 inches × 12 inches = 444 square inches; Area of B = 12 inches × 17 inches = 204 square inches; Area of C = 37 inches × 17 inches = 629 square inches; 444 square inches + 444 square inches + 204 square inches + 204 square inches + 629 square inches + 629 square inches = 2,554 square inches

Pages 28: 3 feet × 2 feet = 6 square feet; 6 feet × 4 feet = 24 square feet

INDEX

CONTENT CONSULTANT

David T. Hughes

David is an experienced mathematics teacher, writer, presenter, and adviser. He serves as a consultant for the Partnership for Assessment of Readiness for College and Careers. David has also worked as the Senior Program Coordinator for the Charles A. Dana Center at The University of Texas at Austin and was an editor and contributor for the *Mathematics Standards in the Classroom* series.